THE EMERGING MEDIA TODDLERS

THE EMERGING MEDIA TODDLERS

Editors: María Dolores Souza & Patricio Cabello

The International Clearinghouse
on Children, Youth and Media

NORDICOM
University of Gothenburg

The Emerging Media Toddlers

Editors:
María Dolores Souza & Patricio Cabello

ISBN 978-91-89471-95-5

Published by:
The International Clearinghouse on Children, Youth and Media

Nordicom
University of Gothenburg
Box 713
SE 405 30 GÖTEBORG
Sweden

Cover by:
Karin Persson

Printed by:
Litorapid Media AB, Göteborg, Sweden, 2010
Environmental certification according to ISO 14001

Contents

Foreword

Interest in babies', toddlers' and preschoolers' media use has grown during recent years, not least within the media industry, which sees possibilities to extend its market by also addressing these already existing and, compared to a few decades ago, previous future consumers. Many families contribute to this process through their own media use as well as by giving electronic and digital media devices to their young children – television sets, computers, music equipment, video games, etc. These very young children are not only socialized into this media environment, but also decide on it themselves in a way that did not exist some 15-20 years ago. The fact that infants and toddlers of today live in a new kind of media landscape with an intricate interrelationship involving themselves, their families and the media industry, also seems to change relations and communications within the family, according to authors María Dolores Souza and Patricio Cabello in this booklet.

However, concerns regarding toddlers' media use are also expressed – among pediatricians who recommend cautious use or even non-use of screen media at the youngest ages, among certain politicians who follow these recommendations, and among those media educators who are of the opinion that media literacy education must start as early as possible.

Little research has been performed on infants' and toddlers' ownership and use of media, especially in the complex context of family and media industry in different societies. Moreover, research on children and media has been much more exuberant and has a longer tradition in wealthy countries, while in developing countries such research is often less common or non-existent. Although research on very young children and media is scarce, this imbalance is valid for that research as well. Thus, the knowledge we have about children and media originates from relatively few countries with specific media situations – and research findings cannot be automatically generalized across borders. Consequently, in most countries there is a great need for research on children and media in the changing local and global media landscape.

The International Clearinghouse on Children, Youth and Media therefore finds it highly relevant to publish this booklet, *The Emerging Media Toddlers*, edited by María Dolores Souza and Patricio Cabello. The booklet provides examples of research and reflections from Latin America (Chile, Mexico and Venezuela), where media technology is rapidly gaining ground even among the poorest children, together with examples of studies and thoughts from countries where children have had access to ICT for a longer time (New Zealand, Sweden and the US). In the contributions, for which we heartily thank the editors, authors and interviewees, we find a diversity in the relations between toddlers and media but also similarities in spite of the countries' economic and cultural differences.

Göteborg, February 2010

Cecilia von Feilitzen   *Ulla Carlsson*
Scientific Coordinator   Director

Introduction: Preschoolers and their Appropriation of Screen Technologies

María Dolores Souza & Patricio Cabello

This booklet brings together articles by and interviews with academics of diverse nationalities who have researched and/or pondered about the relationship today's preschoolers are establishing with screen technologies, especially television.

The profound changes generated by the technological revolution have enabled concepts like "media convergence" and "digital divide" to cross the restrictive barriers of the academic-technical-political world focused on these issues and inhabit the social imaginary of our daily conversations. Likewise, technological developments are playing an increasing role in the socialization of boys and girls in different parts of the world.

As has been highlighted by some authors, research on how children use the media has focused mainly on adolescents and school-aged children,[1] and thus relatively little knowledge has been compiled on the reality of infants, toddlers and preschoolers. This is probably due to at least three main factors:

- There is limited media material aimed at children at this stage of the lifecycle. Furthermore, some countries partially or almost wholly exclude these age groups from audience measurement systems such as ratings.[2]

- The segment in question includes a cohort aged 0 to 2 years, for whom television is discouraged.[3]

- The media consumption of this segment is underestimated both by academia and in the public debate.

Although research and reflection focused on this segment are relatively scarce compared to others, some academic and institutional efforts have produced highly relevant knowledge. These include publications by the Kaiser Family Foundation[4] coordinated by Victoria Rideout, as well as a famous series of articles published in a special edition of *Televizion* by IZI,[5] headed by Maya Götz, and the research work of authors including Daniel Anderson, Eugene Troseth, Tiffany Pempek, Daphna Lemish, Jackie Marsh and others.

While the aforementioned studies have provided important knowledge for the understanding of media consumption among preschoolers, they have mostly been carried out in the developed world. Europe and the United States have a long history of studying media consumption – yet, in developing countries media such as television have undergone a much more recent modernization process, both in the areas of content and consumption, and in associated legislation and public policies. There are obvious differences between the developed and the developing world, not only economic but also cultural. Recognizing this diversity leads to the conclusion that these phenomena need to be analyzed from an intercultural perspective.

Our main focus is on television, and we have used it as a springboard to address various aspects of emerging issues. We have selected and produced material to lay the groundwork for future discussion on the concepts of social diversity in a mediated world. We also address the issue of media literacy as an important variable in the early socialization of children living in the digital age.

The first article on Chilean preschoolers was developed by the Chilean National Television Council's (CNTV) Research Department. It shows how the media, especially television, make up part of the preschoolers' world. It portrays them not only as avid consumers of television and other media, but also as owners of technology and as individuals with a new status within the family group. It aims to encourage a review of the role of the media within the family, as well as of the social uses of audiovisual media and the meanings given to them by an institution as important as the family.

In the second article, Mexican researcher Juan Enrique Huerta presents some reflections on the decision by France's broadcasting regulator CSA to ban the showing of television content specifically aimed at children under three. He offers a rigorous analysis of the arguments supporting the measure, and in doing so provides a critical review of the decision and recent supporting research.

The third article is authored by Mary Jane Shuker and Geoff Lealand, who present an overview of television as a socializing agent in New Zealand. They emphasize the phenomena generated by changes in family composition, increased access to media technology and the cultural transformations of a country whose economic growth has occurred alongside an increased ethnic integration based on migratory processes and the growth of the descendants of the indigenous population, all of which has resulted in a highly heterogeneous preschooler segment. In the context of such an audience, the authors examine the media offers available.

Finally, Olle Findahl's article centers on Internet use. Using Swedish statistical data, he analyzes children's use and knowledge of the Internet, highlighting the average of Internet use among children in the current decade, an Internet use that is nestling down to very young children. In this way he describes and identifies the critical measure that renders this a mass phenomenon in society.

As a complement to these four articles, the booklet includes three interviews with renowned academics.

In the first interview, Daniel Anderson, academic and researcher from Massachusetts University, Amherst, discusses the scope of recent studies on the effects of background television on infant and toddler games. The findings are of great importance, given that they gauge a phenomenon occurring in homes where television is a normal element of the environment and makes up part of the daily routine, which is extremely difficult to study.

In the second interview, Víctor Fuenmayor, Venezuela, presents a comprehensive overview of media literacy, revealing a complex notion of communication based not only on discourse and mental operations, but also on the body, ethnic identity and the organization of social life.

In the final interview, Angharad Valdivia, USA, discusses some ideas regarding the way certain issues such as gender, ethnicity and violence are addressed in children's programming. Valdivia believes it is necessary to produce pro-social content that is more compelling to children than violent programming is. In this context, she points to the inability of commercial television to consider human beings as entities beyond their functions as consumers.

This booklet aims to stimulate the intellectual curiosity of the reader by opening up new topics that have received little attention from the world of academia and as regards public policies involving very young children.

Notes

1. See: Singer, D. "To watch or not to watch – that is the (research) question. Effect of early TV viewing, and an analysis of favourite preschool programmes", *Televizion*. 20/2007/E, pp. 20-24. Also recommended are meta-analysis studies such as Thakkar, R.R., Garrison, M.M., & Christakis, D.A. (2006) "A systematic review for the effects of television viewing by infants and preschoolers", *Pediatrics*, Vol. 118, No. 5, pp. 2025-2031.
2. In the case of the United States, Nielsen's minimum age group for ratings is two years, while in Chile the minimum age is four.
3. American Academy of Pediatrics. "Children, adolescents and television" (Policy statement). *Pediatrics* Vol. 107, No. 2 February 2001, pp. 423-426 http://aappolicy.aappublications.org/cgi/reprint/pediatrics;107/2/423.pdf
4. See: Kaiser Family Foundation (2003) "Zero to Six: Electronic Media in the Lives of Infants, Toddlers and Preschoolers". USA.
5. Götz, M. (ed.) "Television for Beginners", *Televizion*, 20/2007/E.

Report 0 to 5
Chilean Preschoolers and the Media[1]

María Dolores Souza & Patricio Cabello

Technology is changing rapidly, and the availability of information technologies in Latin American countries is spreading across different socio-economic groups. In Chile and Argentina, this includes the poorest children and their homes. Mexico, Brazil and Venezuela have a middle-range penetration of new media and technologies in the homes of children and adolescents, and currently in a less privileged position are Peru and Colombia.[2] Additionally, new generations are incorporating the technological changes at a very early age, making them part of their lives. Media and other technologies are becoming social experiences for toddlers and babies.

Most of the information available on this phenomenon comes from developed countries,[3] and it is still quite unknown what the situation is in Latin America, particularly Chile, where the technological revolution has had an enormous impact. However, according to the study "Interactive Generation in Iberoamerica",[4] Chilean adolescents have a better situation than their peers in the Latin American region when it comes to the availability of different technological goods at home.

Current societal changes have led us to question child developmental theories, because technology and media – old and new – may bear influence, foment or inhibit normal aspects of child development in many ways. Some experts have even said that technology is also a content,[5] a social experience made possible through technology – each technology with its specific way of making it possible to build a social experience within a culture.

The following text is a selection of the main results of two studies[6] aimed at gathering information on the daily life of children under six years of age in Chile.

The first part covers the findings regarding the group of two- to five-year-olds, focusing on how the media becomes part of everyday family life as a significant factor in socialization, the volume of media consumption and the skills for using new technology. The second part is a summary of the results on the group of six-month-old babies to 23-month-old toddlers. In this latter study we were able to observe an increasingly early access of babies to the media, particularly television, due to their mothers' viewing habits.

Children aged two to five years

The world of preschoolers revolves around the family environment; therefore, to understand their relationship with media it is important to observe family behavior, consumption habits, and how the family uses media in everyday interaction.

The first-mentioned study[7] shows that one of Chilean children's main family activities at two to five years of age is watching TV (96.7%), along with having lunch/dinner (97.8%) and talking (97.7%). So, we can assume that television viewing is also a way of relating among family members, such as eating and talking. This is what ethnographic observation revealed: that watching TV is an important part of the parent/child relationship in this age group.

Preschoolers entering the digital era interact with their surroundings, which include technological artefacts, and this refers not only to the use of technology, but also to ownership: 49.6 percent of children aged two to five own at least one technological device that all family members recognize as belonging to him or her, and not to the household in general.

Surprising as it might seem, preschoolers in lower income groups own more technological devices than do their peers in higher income groups. This leads us to believe that in high-income families, these artifacts were purchased long ago for the house, including parents and peers, while in lower income groups, access to these goods has been more recent and they were therefore purchased as gifts for their child. This might be especially the case with computers, which Chilean society recognizes as a cultural and educational benefit.

Most preschoolers of high, middle and middle-low socioeconomic status (SES) and who own a TV set have it in their bedrooms. Children of low SES and in extremely poor families have their sets mainly in their parents' bedroom or in a bedroom shared with other siblings. Houses are very small in these socio-economic groups, sometimes just a single room made of wood for families of three, five or more members, but children nevertheless know which television set or other objects belong to them or to others. Though these children are very young, parents seem to believe they have the right to own certain technologi-cal goods, like any other toy. Some parents say that it helps children develop a sense of responsibility about their belongings, with some comparing it to having a pet. So there is a space in the house where kids can keep and use their media and technological goods, even if the house is only a crowded single room for all family members.[8]

Seemingly, watching television is the main daily activity of preschoolers: 84.7 percent of the parents say that their child watches TV every day – and only a small minority – 3.4 percent – say that their child never watches. Music also stands out as one of the young children's main media-related activities (34.3%

listen to it every day). Surprisingly, the youngest members of this age group, particularly girls, are those who listen to music the most. The use of highly sophisticated technology such as video games, online games, chats and other alternatives on the Internet is not yet a habit among preschoolers, but their use begins in early childhood.[9] The natural barrier for using technology is the skills required to do so. Such is the case with computers, which are used three times more by four- to five-year-olds than by two- to three-year-olds. On the other hand, there is a clear relationship between socioeconomic status and the use of technology, with the high SES standing out over the rest, due to a greater availability of these goods. In the case of computer use, parents of higher SES have more than one computer at home, but on the other hand may care less about damages.

Children acquire autonomy in the use of technology as they get older, with no differences between boys and girls. This is a striking finding, because earlier studies[10] have revealed gender differences with regard to interest in and attraction to technology. The use of technology includes MP3, portable CDs and music equipment at home, which, compared to television, require basic skills whereas other devices or services, such as the Internet and video games, require more advanced skills.

Almost one-third of the children (29.2%) between four and five years of age use computers without any assistance, whereas only 6.3 percent of two- to three-year-olds can do so.

It is worth noting the high number of children between two and five who do not need help operating a DVD (39.6%). Apparently today, movies are used in the same way as storybooks were in the past: we were able to observe that, similar to what happens when parents read from storybooks, children want to see the same movie over and over again.

Parents believe that television is one of the most entertaining activities for their children. On average, children two to five years of age watch television 3.5 hours a day. There are some differences among socioeconomic groups, with middle-low and low SES watching one hour more on the whole. Children watch TV mostly in the company of others (average 2.8 hours) and little alone (0.7 hours), mainly in the mornings and afternoons. As expected, children in this age group watch almost no television after the 10 p.m. watershed.

The average time that the television set is turned on in the home is 6.8 hours, with significant differences among different SES. The lower the SES, the longer the television is turned on (7.4 hours in the lowest SES homes compared to 4.0 hours in the higher SES homes). These results reveal a high exposure to *background TV*[11] that is part of the family environment, particularly in low-income households. Ethnographic data show that young children's television consumption and play are sometimes merged as a sole activity.

Children who go to school tend to watch less TV – one hour less – than those who stay at home. The study shows no significant time differences between watching alone and with others. This finding stresses the fact that young children want to be in the company of others and watch television so as to be with their mothers, other caretakers or siblings. Other ethnographic studies by our research department show the same result. The programs preschoolers watch are mainly targeted at adults, older children and youth, because about 60 percent of Chilean families have only access to open TV – no cable or satellite – which offers very few programs targeted at children: a mere 7 percent of broadcasting time, with only two programs for preschoolers.[12]

Most parents of children aged two to six (64%) consider the amount of television their children watch to be adequate.[13] On the other hand, parents who feel their children watch too much television (4%) respond that the children watch an average of six hours a day.

Young children tend to decide what to watch on television; according to their parents this happens always (36.2%) or almost always (25.6%) as compared to never (32.1%) or almost never (6.1%). This result is interesting, because this was absolutely not the case 15 years ago in Chile. Young children depended on the choice of older siblings or adults to be able to watch television. Today, decision-making by preschoolers is broadly accepted with respect to the use of technologies and in other fields as well.[14]

When asked about their children's favorite programs, parents mention 60 different ones: most frequently *Barney*, *Lazy Town*, and *Hi Five*. These are fiction series with human characters; two of the three programs include adults and/or teenagers. The three programs seek to interact with the audience and promote healthy behavior through models. *Barney* is favored among younger children and *Lazy Town* among girls. Cartoons are widely preferred by all (43.2%), followed by children's series (32.8%). There are some slight differences according to gender: Boys tend to like cartoons the most, while girls prefer series with human actors.

These young children prefer programs targeted at their age group, and in second place, programs aimed at "tweens", that is, eight- to 13-year-olds. Yet gender differences are striking at this age range. Girls (32.6%) more often than boys (24.3%) prefer the programs targeted at their age group, whereas boys (36.6%) more often than girls (18.1%) prefer programs aimed at tweens.

Parents of two- to five-year-olds do not seem to be concerned about violent content on television, especially when it comes to adult programs.[15] Some parents do perceive that their children react with fear to violent cartoons (12.8 %), but cartoons are the exception – no other programs or characters, fictional or real, are mentioned. On the other hand, most parents say their children imitate what they see on television. More than half, 53.9 percent, say that they imitate cartoons; 47.9 percent say they imitate musical groups; and 36.5 percent say they imitate the hosts of children's programs. Imitation seems to be more common among boys than girls, according to the parents. Our experience in the field tells us that these are not long-lasting behaviors, but nevertheless, the gender difference could be interesting to investigate further.

Children under two

The results of the second study[16] show that the main activities of children under two years of age are related in one way or another to media and technologies: Mothers say that their babies and toddlers listen to music everyday (89%); play with toys (86%); watch free-to-air TV (76%); dance (74%); sing (63%); watch paid TV (42%); ride a tricycle (32%); play with pets (28%); and play video games (6%) .

Compared to the results of children aged two to five, infants watch somewhat less TV, and mostly in the company of others. Still, babies' and toddlers' amount of viewing is high – over two hours a day – especially considering the current debate about babies and TV viewing.[17] There are no significant time differences according to age: Toddlers aged 19 to 23 months watch an average of 2.86 hours a day, while babies aged 7 to 18 months watch a little over two hours daily. The difference lies in the babies' tending to watch television accompanied by others, while the toddlers spend about one hour watching alone. These results are similar to those in other countries. A study in the US revealed[18] that about 40 percent of 3 month-old infants watch television, DVDs or videos regularly, while 90 percent of two-year-old toddlers do the same. Furthermore, the same study shows that children under one year of age watch an average of one hour a day, and two-year-olds 1.5 hours.

Other results of CNTV studies[19] – i.e., on schoolchildren aged 8-13 – show that TV viewing among children depends on the amount of time the TV set is turned on; but in the case of babies and toddlers, television consumption is not directly related to the amount of time the TV is on. Age appears to be a more dominant factor in TV viewing related to children's capacity to pay attention to the screen.

When mothers stay at home, children under two watch more TV (2.14 hours a day)[20] than do their peers whose mothers work outside the home (1.8 hours). This is most likely due to the fact that children want to spend time with their mothers as mentioned previously and, thus, do what their mothers are doing.[21] Another hypothesis is, of course, that mothers leave their children in front of the TV screen in order to do chores.

Children have a very early encounter with television, and this phenomenon is not always perceived as such by their parents. For this reason, we asked mothers who were currently breastfeeding their baby what they did while nursing. The main answers were "talk to the child" (91%) or "sing" to it (72%), followed by "watch TV" (56%). This is an important result, because breastfeeding is an experience of primary contact with the mother.

Concluding remarks

Today's preschoolers in Chile seem more precocious than those of the previous decade. They are more assertive and they have – through media – developed new abilities that enable them to have their voice heard at home. In this sense,

17

we see a qualitative change in how families communicate, toward a more horizontal and less hierarchic manner. Media and new technologies available at home contribute to this phenomenon, allowing children to get a greater glimpse of the adult world, which thus loses part of its mystery. Television portrays the experiences and conflicts of different generations, which somehow bridges the gap and demystifies the world of older children, teenagers and adults. On the other hand, being native technological users, young kids are ahead of their parents regarding familiarity with the media environment.

Of course, economic growth, democracy and globalization also play a role in shaping these changes within the family, but media and new technologies contribute by challenging old family structures and culture. Studying toddlers' TV consumption as well as their use of other technological devices has made it possible for us to observe these changes that might also occur in Argentina, as well as in middle-range technological households in other Latin American countries. If, in the past, technological devices belonged to the parents and young children were not allowed to play around with them, today's parents are making every effort – even in the poorest family households – to create a real or symbolic space for preschoolers within the home so as to enable them to access technology.

The good news about this is that children gain self-confidence and develop new skills that will be relevant in their school years and later in life.

The bad news is that parents of toddlers and babies are seemingly unaware of the current debate on the amount of television children under two or three years of age should be viewing. The other piece of bad news is that they overlook the problem of their very young children watching violence and other harmful content on television. Though parents are very concerned about violent content when it comes to their children aged eight to 13, they are not so with toddlers. This fact makes us aware of the importance of media education in this country to facilitate and better understand the importance of the use of television, DVDs, video games and other technologies among toddlers.

To foster and demand quality content – over any screen or device – we need quality consumers.

Notes

1. This research received support from McCann Erickson Chile and had as its advisor psychologist Víctor Martínez.
2. *La generación interactiva en Iberoamerica: niños y adolescentes ante las pantallas*. Fundación Telefonica, 2008, Spain. This research was conducted in the seven countries mentioned in the text. It compares the households of children and youth ten to 18 years old on 14 media and technological goods.
3. For a thorough analysis, see: Rideout, Victoria et al. (2006) *The media family: electronic media in the lives of infants, toddlers, preschoolers and their parents*. Kaiser Family Foundation, USA.
4. Op. cit. Fundación Telefonica, 2008, Spain. Chile is above average on 13 of the 14 items studied; Argentina is above average on 11 items.
5. The International Institute of Communications. 2009 Annual Conference. Montreal. www.iicom. org

6. National Television Council (CNTV) (2007) *Report 0 to 5: Chilean Preschoolers/Toons*. Research Department, National Television Council, Chile. Full report in Spanish at: http://www.cntv.cl/medios/Publicaciones/libroToons2007.pdf

7. The first study was based on a design that combined: a) interviews with experts; b) 400 face-to-face interviews with parents of children aged two to five from five different socio-economic groups (including extreme poverty) in Santiago; c) a period of ethnographic observation in ten households and five preschools, with the same stratification as in the survey.

8. In Chile, extreme-poverty households are identified by small wooden houses that do not have separate rooms. The bathroom is the only space that is separated from the rest, and is sometimes inside and sometimes outside.

9. Evidently, when technologies are available to the child.

10. See: Maria Cristina Lasagni "Genere Femminile e Nuovi Media Domestici: le famiglie e l'adozione del'innovazione delle nuove tecnologie della comunicazione" 1997. Centro Studi San Salvador – Telecom Italia (in Italian). See also National Television Council of Chile 1994, 1995, 1997. However, these studies never focused on this issue because Chilean households had little access to technology at the time. See: *Consumo Televisivo Infantil: Estudio de Observación Participante*: www.cntv.cl (in Spanish).

11. There is recent proof that "background television reduces play episode length and focused attention" among children three years old and younger. Background TV is defined as "adult content that is largely incomprehensible to a very young child and to which they ordinarily pay little cumulative attention". See: Schmidt, M.E., Pempek, T.A., Kirkorian, H.L, Frankenfield Lund, A. and Anderson, D.R. "The effects of background television on the toy play behavior of very young children". *Child Development*. July/August 2008, Volume 79, Number 4, pp. 1137-1151.

12. In Chile, there are six free-to-air national channels. The historical percentage of children's programs was around 12%, which is already very low. In 2009 it is around 7%, with only two programs aimed at preschool children. Official data of the CNTV, Chilean Television Council Regulator (to be published).

13. As mentioned before, the average of TV viewing is 3.5 hours a day (alone or in the company of others).

14. See full report (op.cit.)

15. This was a surprising result, given that parents of older children express significant concern about the negative influence of television.

16. The second study consisted of a telephone survey to 250 mothers of children between six and 23 months of age, from five different socioeconomic groups.

17. Also, the American Academy of Pediatrics (AAP) recommends no screen viewing for children under two and after that age, the viewing time recommendation is one to two hours a day. See: http://pediatrics.aappublications.org/cgi/content/full/108/5/1222

18. Rideout, Victoria et al. (2006) *The media family: electronic media in the lives of infants, toddlers, preschoolers and their parents*. Kaiser Family Foundation, USA.

19. See: *Consumo Televisivo Infantil: Estudio de Observación Participante*. CNTV: 1995 www.cntv.cl; and *ConsumoTelevisio Infantil. El caso del cable. Un studio cualitativo de observación participante*. CNTV: 1997, www.cntv.cl

20. Watching TV with others at home has been called *the ritual function of TV*, in which the set brings the family together. The child's desire to spend time with their parents leads the child to watch programs that are not necessarily of their interest, such as news programs.

21. This result appears systematically in our research.

Protection des mineurs in France
A Research-based Discussion on the Effects of Television on Children Less than Three Years of Age

Juan Enrique Huerta

Consider a typical family with an infant in an average country in Europe or the Americas. As Nielsen reports have frequently pointed out, television constitutes a kind of fourth family member, because a television set is available, and turned on, in almost every home in these countries. The average family with at least one child less than three years of age at home has just two possibilities for using this TV set. The first is watching a program that mommy and/or daddy prefer, and the second is watching an "educational" program, like *Barney* or *Baby Mozart*. Of course, it is theoretically possible to turn off the television, but from research data is not apparent that this choice is frequent among 21st-century parents. This extraordinary change in daily life patterns is what the broadcast authority in France expects that parents do as a result of its last measure in child protection, or *protection des mineurs*.

In July 2008, the broadcast authority in France told the country's channels not to market television shows as suitable for children less than three years of age. Citing health experts who say that interaction with people is crucial to early childhood development and that viewing television at a young age poses risks, the Conseil Supérieur de l'Audiovisuel (CSA) is trying to block such programming by preventing the channels from broadcasting it. In this way, the French broadcast authority is mirroring and even going beyond the American Academy of Pediatrics, who in 1999 started urging parents to avoid exposure to screen media for children less than two years of age. Despite the recommendations of pediatricians, both argued effects and policy measures deserve an inspection from a research perspective. The goal of this piece is to briefly analyze the measures taken by the French government and discuss some research findings that lead us to be suspicious about the effectiveness of the Délibération n° 2008-85, which is supposed to protect children less than three years of age from the effects of television.

Protection des mineurs: CSA's Délibération n° 2008-85

On July 22, 2008, the CSA agreed on Délibération 2008-85 (Conseil Supérieur de l'Audiovisuel, 2008). The published text of this policy covers a consultation among health and child development experts, who apparently agreed that infants' exposure to television is replacing human interaction. The experts also agreed that human interaction is needed for child development. According to the same experts, whose names and credentials were not published, exposure to television favors passivity and anxiety, sleep and concentration disturbances, and a reduction in language acquisition.

The CSA states that

scientific fundamentals about children's cognitive and psychological development tend to conclude that television shows designed for infants have no beneficial effects on psychomotor or affective development. On the contrary, the available research suggests that television consumption threatens the development of thinking, imagination, and feelings of integration.[1]

The policy measures contained in Deliberation 2008-85 include two main points. The first is the restriction to broadcast any show geared to children less than three years of age. The second is the beginning of a broad television campaign to discourage the consumption of television by these children, by informing the population about risks in development and trying to encourage parents to substitute television exposure with parent-child interaction. This campaign intends to encourage turning off television at home.

The CSA's deliberation was published in August 2008. A mere few months later, of course, it is too early to evaluate whether the overall policy is working, but a research-based discussion is worthy because it was needed in July in Paris to help the CSA's committee in the decision-making process.[2] In essence, the CSA wrote a policy to protect French children based on French health and development arguments that can be summarized as follows: a) greater interaction with adults, mainly parents or main caregivers, leads to greater physical, psychomotor, cognitive, and affective child development; b) television is replacing human interaction; c) exposure to television has several negative effects in terms of child development; d) exposure to television has no beneficial effects in terms of child development; e) the overall child development may improve if parents turn off the television at home; f) parents will turn off the television if governments publicize that their children can be harmed if they do not. These arguments will be reviewed briefly in the following sections.

CSA's arguments: What we know

The evidence that greater interaction with parents or main caregivers leads to several positive effects constitutes a milestone in child development research. There is no controversy about this, and the literature will not be discussed in this piece mainly due to the limited space available. Thus, point a) ("greater interaction with adults, mainly parents or main caregivers, leads to greater physical, psychomotor, cognitive, and affective child development") will not be analyzed here and is considered plausible.

Otherwise, media textbooks have plenty of quotes documenting that in the history of media technology, any new technology has faced the criticism that technology is replacing human interaction and isolating human beings. Despite this, human beings are more in touch with any new technology, and this criticism receives no more than a complicit smile among the analyst community when it is evaluated. This is why the second argument, b) ("television is replacing human interaction"), is not addressed here. Arguments about the negative and positive effects of television on child development deserve a more elaborate analysis.

c) "Exposure to television has negative effects in terms of child development"

As regards the third argument – see also the heading above – two kinds of negative television effects have been cited in the CSA's deliberation, namely learning and emotional problems. Indeed, one of the oldest concerns regarding children viewing television is how it might affect a child's school performance. In the case of preschoolers, this concern is that it can affect cognitive development, especially language acquisition. As Lemish (2007) documented, in the research literature there are three broad hypotheses about negative effects of television on learning: 1) displacement, or the probability that television may displace activities like playing with parents or toys; 2) information processing, or the probability that television affects children's cognitive abilities; 3) gratification, or the probability that children find learning from television more gratifying in comparison to more traditional learning tools, thus developing positive attitudes toward television and negative attitudes toward traditional learning approaches.

The displacement hypothesis was popular and tested long ago, when households with and without televisions could still be compared. The classic book by Schramm, Lyle & Parker (1961), *Television in the Lives of Our Children,* presented empirical evidence that television viewing displaced playtime in general in the USA. As Valkenburg (2001) has noted, some research has pointed out that more playtime relates to imaginative play, which is why it can be stated that less playtime derives less imagination. It has been supported in the literature that the arrival of television resulted in a decrease in children's imagination (i.e., Harrison & Williams, 1986).

One typical way to measure the development of cognitive abilities has been visualization. The typical experiment compares the speed at which children solve problems, when those problems are presented in different formats. For instance, the problems can be presented to compare audiovisual, audio, or print formats (drawings). A different solution lies in comparing screening to face-to-face problems, i.e., showing the children how to solve problems by watching a video or through a window. Frequently, young children are found to evoke solutions rapidly if they learn through verbal solutions (i.e., following directions directly from instructors) rather than if they learn through screens (Greenfield & Beagles-Roos, 1988; Schmidt & Anderson, 2007). The theory behind this is that young children can visualize solutions in their minds when they are trying to solve problems, as a result of the medium used as a stimulus. The children then develop creative thinking tools and overall cognitive capabilities.

What about the anxiety problems cited in the CSA's deliberation? Well, literally hundreds of correlational studies have found that violence on television is related to anxiety and arousal in children. Cantor has followed this kind of research question for more than 30 years (e.g., Cantor, 2003), and has consistently proven that violence on television causes anxiety, aggression, desensitization, and interpersonal hostility in children.

Other problems not cited in the CSA's deliberation include obesity and sleep disruption. Medical evidence suggests that obesity and sleep disruption are correlated to how many hours children watch television. An example is a survey of the parents of almost 500 young children in the United States revealing that the amount of child television viewing (especially at bedtime) and having a television in one's own bedroom were significantly related to the frequency of sleep disturbances (Taveras et al., 2008).

d) "Exposure to television has no beneficial effects in terms of child development"

The fourth argument d) – see the heading – is by far the most crucial point in the CSA's deliberation. If watching television has only negative effects and no beneficial ones on children and their families, we would have to throw television in the trash, if such a thing were possible. However, the only thing we as scholars can be sure of from research on media effects is that the evidence is contradictory and complex.

Actually, the focus of media studies has changed and only a few scholars are talking about effects, basically in psychology departments. As Lemish (2007) remembers in her well written and comprehensive book on children and media, a powerful change in the question "How does television affect children?" was to ask "What are children doing with television?". A great deal of dust has fallen since the 70s, when such a question was developed.

According to the CSA's deliberation, television inhibits the development of language. This is not a research-based tale. Indeed, the best example of not so negative effects on young children comes from language acquisition. A research question to test this sentence should operationalize television and also the development of language; it is not easy to do this.

24

First, we have to distinguish between foreground and background television, as Anderson & Pempek (2005) have recommended. According to those authors,

> foreground television is programming to which very young children overtly attend in a sustained manner [...] programming designed for young children and is presumably at least partially comprehensible to them. Background television consists of programming to which very young children pay little overt attention. Such programming is generally not produced for children and would be largely incomprehensible to them. The distinction between foreground and background television is relevant because foreground television could in principle be educational for very young children and have a positive impact in addition to or instead of the presumed negative impact (Anderson & Pempek, 2005, p. 506)

Foreground television is intended to be exposed to young children. Background television is not.

Second, we have to distinguish whether we would understand the development of language as the development of grammar or vocabulary. A more elaborated issue, of course not interesting to the French but to many other countries in the world, is whether we will refer to the development of a first or a second language.

Linebarger & Walker (2005) showed that it is also important to distinguish between different television content. Potter (e.g., Potter & Chang, 1990) has demonstrated that television is not a whole, but that different programs affect different people differently. Linebarger & Walker showed that this is exactly the same for infants and toddlers. At 30 months of age, watching *Dora the Explorer*, *Blue's Clues*, *Arthur*, *Clifford*, or *Dragon Tales* resulted in greater vocabulary words and higher expressive language (i.e., single and multiple-word utterances); watching *Teletubbies* was related to fewer vocabulary words and less expressive language scores; and viewing *Barney and Friends* was related to fewer vocabulary words and expressive language. Linebarger & Walker controlled child and family characteristics, including the quality and quantity of stimulation and support available to a child in the home environment. Control variables also included the total amount of TV exposure. Total viewing, including adult programming, was associated with reduced vocabulary but slightly increased expressed language. In general, this research suggested that early television viewing may have both positive and negative impacts on language development, depending on content.

Similar results were found by Krcmar, Grela & Lin (2007). They found that toddlers were able to learn new words from a televised model if the model used strategies known to evoke language in live interaction situations. In contrast, toddlers who watched *Teletubbies* (a program with poor language models and little elicitation of participation or communication) were not able to learn new words. A conclusion emerging from this paper is that specific language-promoting characteristics incorporated into televised programs or used by televised models can be successful in helping toddlers learn language.

Saying that television does not have any beneficial effects on young children constitutes a direct attack on *Sesame Street*, the top institution of media for children. Sesame Workshop, the *Sesame Street*'s producer home, has worked for 40 years with the aim of producing effective educational programs that are enjoyable through professional cooperation among educational, psychological and TV-producer experts. Currently, it is estimated that more than 120 million children in 140 countries around the world watch *Sesame Street* regularly. Estimates of viewing habits in the USA suggest that about 95 percent of children are already viewing *Sesame Street* on a regular basis at the time they are three years old. It is true that the evidence is not yet conclusive about its educational objectives. Still, a good number of research papers are showing beneficial effects in terms of infants' and toddlers' educational achievements. A general conclusion on educational television has been stated by Lemish (2007):

> Children who watch attractive educational television programs learn whatever it is they are taught (p. 176).

Parents will turn off the television

The last two sentences in the CSA's deliberation are e) "Child development may improve if parents turn off the television off at home", and f) "Parents will turn off the television if governments publicize that their children can be harmed if they do not". These sentences relate to an outcome in contradiction with the CSA's decision, which is the power of families to regulate what is good or bad for children. In essence, the French government has replaced family freedom to make home decisions because the government considers French families to be unable to make decisions on their own concerning the television exposure of their children.

The positive or negative influence of television on child development, as the research quoted above has revealed, depends on television content. It is not true that television overall can be judged identically, but different content affects different people differently. This is apparent from the research on adults, and it is also apparent from the research on infants and toddlers. One more research-based statement is that the influence of television on infants and toddlers also depends on their reception context, such as the home environments where these young children watch television. The research shows that several variables moderate the way a child views television as well as the influence of television. These variables include socioeconomic status, educational materials at home, parents' education, parents' political attitudes, and parental supervision of children's television viewing (e.g., Lemish, 2007).

True, research findings suggest that parents and children use their time best when they share time on activities that do not include television exposure, like playing. Although parents may know this, it is also true that it is difficult to do it. Consider a modern family in a Western country. The parents have grown up with the television turned on just like any other family member. Modern cultural studies research states that television establishes a daily life rhythm, acting as a big, monotonous wall clock (including a clock). It may be dangerous, yes; however, we know that there are dangerous things in almost every meal, and yet we continue consuming things like Diet Coke.

French parents will not turn off the television or dramatically change their daily life habits. What we know about human behavior suggests that they simply will not have educational, foreground television available to watch. French children will thus view background television, disruptive adult television not suitable for them, which is exactly the kind of television that previous research has concluded may damage child development.

Notes

1. This is a non-authorized translation by the author of this article.
2. This research note was written at the end of 2008.

References

Anderson, D.R., & Pempek, T.A. (2005) 'Television and Very Young Children', *American Behavioral Scientist, 48*, pp. 505-522.

Cantor, J. (2003) 'Media Violence and its Effect on Aggression: Assessing the Scientific Evidence', *Journalism and Mass Communication Quarterly, 80*(2), p. 468.

Conseil Supérieur de l'Audiovisuel (2008) Délibération du 22 juillet 2008 visant à protéger les enfants de moins de 3 ans des effets de la télévision. Retrieved October 12, 2008 from http://www.csa.fr/infos/textes/textes_detail.php?id=126993

Greenfield, P., & Beagles-Roos, J. (1988) 'Radio vs. Television: Their Cognitive Impact on Children of Different Socio-economic and Ethnic Groups', *Journal of Communication, 38*(2), pp. 71-82.

Harrison, L.F., & Williams, T.M. (1986) 'Television and Cognitive Development', in T.M. Williams (ed.), The Impact of Television Commercial Form and Commercial Placement on Children's Social Behavior and Attention, *Child Development, 53*, pp. 611-619.

Krcmar, M., Grela, B., & Lin, K. (2007) 'Can Toddlers Learn Vocabulary from Television? An Experimental Approach', *Media Psychology, 10*(1), pp. 41-63.

Lemish, D. (2007) *Children and Television: A Global Perspective*. Malden, MA: Blackwell Publishing.

Linebarger, D.L., & Walker, D. (2005) 'Infants' and Toddlers' Television Viewing and Language Outcomes', *American Behavioral Scientist, 48*(5), pp. 624-645.

Potter, W.J., & Chang, I.C. (1990) 'Television Exposure Measures and the Cultivation Hypothesis', *Journal of Broadcasting & Electronic Media, 34*(3), pp. 313- 333.

Schmidt, M.E., & Anderson, D.R. (2007) 'Two-year-olds' object retrieval based on television: Testing a perceptual account'. *Media Psychology, 9,* 389-409.

Schramm, W., Lyle, J., & Parker, E.B. (1961) *Television in the Lives of Our Children*. Stanford, CA: Stanford University Press.

Taveras, E.M., Rifas-Shiman, S.L., Oken, E., Gunderson, E.P., & Gillman, M.W. (2008) 'Short Sleep Duration in Infancy and Risk of Childhood Overweight', *Archives of Pediatrics & Adolescent Medicine, 162*(4), pp. 305-311.

Valkenburg, P.M. (2001) 'Television and the Child's Developing Imagination', in Singer, D.G., & Singer, J.L. (eds.) *Handbook of Children and the Media*. Thousand Oaks, CA: SAGE, pp. 121-134.

Growing Up With Television in the South Pacific

Mary Jane Shuker & Geoff Lealand

Television is an experience that is shared by most children across the world.

> Children of both genders and all ages, races, religions, classes, and geographical regions of the world watch television on a regular basis, enjoy it tremendously, and learn more about the world from it than from any other socializing agent.[1]

Children aged 14 years and under who are in a family situation are classified as 'dependent children' in New Zealand.[2] As in most other industrialized countries, these young children are now being raised in a variety of social arrangements, with a gradual shift away from extended families to nuclear families and, increasingly, to more diverse family structures. Since the 1970s, one of the key changes has been the significant shift away from two-parent families to one-parent families.[3] It is highly likely, therefore, that many children will grow up in New Zealand households where one of the biological parents is absent.

Step-families have also become widespread in New Zealand. According to Pool, Dharmalingam & Sceats, reconstituted and blended families, by the 1980s and 1990s, had become far more common and are one of the more important changes to the nuclear family.[4]

Research suggests that along with more diverse family structures, young children today are more likely to be confined to the home environment and be less independently mobile in comparison to twenty years ago. Parents now spend a smaller amount of time with their children but try to compensate for this by providing increasing economic resources to the rearing of their children.[5] In relation to family media environments, nearly all New Zealand children's homes have the following:

> television (99.5%), cellphone (96%), radio (95%) and DVD player (92%). Most homes have a computer (88%), video (79%), digital camera (75%), games console for TV (66%) and MP3 player (56%). Relatively fewer homes have a decoder (47%), a hand-held games console (35%) or a camcorder (34%).[6]

The majority of 4 to 5 year olds in the study watched television (95%) and video tapes or DVDs (85%). Of these children one-third watched recorded television programmes while one in five used the internet (20%). Interestingly, children who lived with just one adult were less likely to use the internet (3% in comparison to 20% of all 4 to 5 year olds). Differences were also evident with 4 to 5 year old children from higher socio-demographic groups being more likely than children from lower groups to watch videos or DVDs.[7]

Children's lives have also altered due to changes in the compulsory and non-compulsory education sectors. The years of compulsory schooling were extended to 16 in 2008. For the non-compulsory early childhood sector, increasing numbers of young children are now attending a service of some kind. In 2007 there were 190,097 young children enrolled, a growth of 6.1 percent (10,906) since 2003.[8] Particularly noteworthy, is that an increasing proportion of 1 and 2 year olds are now attending early childhood services.[9]

These children, along with those who do not attend early childhood services, speak a diversity of different languages, eat a variety of foods, play diverse games, wear dissimilar clothes and may face very different challenges in their daily lives. New Zealand has become significantly more ethnically mixed over the last decade, due to an increase in immigration from a broad range of countries.[10] During the 1990s, for example, the ratio of the population who identified themselves as belonging to an Asian ethnic group increased by 13 percent. Over the same decade, higher fertility rates and comparatively young age profiles resulted in the Maori population rising by 21 percent and Pacific peoples by 39 percent.[11] Within all this range of possibilities, the vast majority of young children watch television.

Local programming

Preschoolers, or under-fives, in New Zealand (some 335,000 children, out of total of 4.2 million citizens)[12] are growing up in a television environment which continues to provide specialist programming for this special audience. Such programming includes imports from the United Kingdom (prestigious series such as *Teletubbies* and *In the Night Garden*), US-originating animation, imports dubbed into *te reo Maori* (for Maori preschoolers), and a continuing strand of locally-produced programming.

A recent arrival on the New Zealand production scene is Weta Workshop, the Wellington-based production house internationally renowned for its special effects contributions to *The Lord of the Rings* trilogy (2002-2005). In 2008, the Weta-produced animation series *Jane and the Dragon*, co-produced with the Canadian YTV Network, and based on the books by Australian children's writer Martin Baynton, was screening on American television (on NBC's Qubo channel and Spanish-language Telemundo) as well as in New Zealand. According to its Academy Award-winning producer Richard Taylor:

Children are a critically discerning audience. There's no gray area at all. They either like it or they don't. Also, there's an incredible need for extreme care to be taken around the moral compass that you build into your show if it's for children.[13]

Taylor and Weta Workshop are also involved in another preschool series *The Wots-Wots*, due to screen on ABC (Australia) Children's Television in April 2007, and on Television New Zealand in March 2009. Similar concerns about the particular emotional and cognitive needs of the very young also shapes the endeavours of other New Zealand producers of preschool programming, motivated by a desire to encourage "preschoolers to follow their dreams".[14]

Weta Workshop are primarily oriented towards the global market for pre-school programming but there are smaller production companies providing for the particular needs of New Zealand children. The Maori Television Service, which operates two nationally-available channels, puts particular emphasis on language (*te reo Maori*) learning and cultural awareness through its own *Manu Rere* (screening weekday afternoons) and imported series, such as *Pippi Long-stocking* and *Di-Gata Defender*, which are dubbed into Maori.

The scheduling of preschool television in New Zealand is clustered in the early morning (6 a.m.-8.30 a.m.) and weekday afternoon (3 p.m-5 p.m.) slots mix of preschool and primary school age programming. Locally-produced, studio-based series such as *The Go Show* and *Sticky TV* (both Pickled Possum Productions) appear in such time-slots, on Television New Zealand's TV2, and TV3 (owned by Australian-based private equity Ironbridge Capital).

The dominant pay-TV service in New Zealand is Sky Network Television, owned and operated by New Zealand-based Independent News Limited (44% owned by News Corporation), currently in 46 percent of New Zealand households (June 2008). Sky provides more a myriad of terrestrial and digital satellite channels, which includes The Disney Channel (including Disney Playhouse), Cartoon Network and Nickelodeon. Such channels are primarily overseas feeds, with minimal local content.

Other prime slots for preschool television are Saturday and Sunday mornings between 6 a.m. and 8 a.m. A unique facet of television in New Zealand is that these preschool slots are advertising free and commerce-free zones which are rare in a television environment that is dominated by advertising breaks, sponsorship and programme naming rights in all other areas of the schedule. As part of agreement reached between advertisers, advertising agencies, the Broadcasting Standards Authority and free-to-air television channels, The Children's Television Policies stipulates that:

- Advertising, sponsorship or prize packs are not allowed during pre-school television programming.
- The broadcasters currently define these programming times as:
TV2:	Monday-Friday	8.35-9.35am
TV3:	Saturday	6.30-7.00pm
Maori Television:	Monday-Friday	3.30-4.30pm
	Saturday	4.00-5.00pm

- By law there are no advertisements on Sunday morning until midday.[15]

Another unique aspect of New Zealand television environment is that most locally-produced preschool programming is funded out of the public purse, through the independent, state-funded agency New Zealand On Air (for free-to-air channels) and Te Mangai Paho (for the Maori Television Service). A small base of independent production companies has developed in wake of this "ring-fencing" and preschoolers continue to be catered for as a special audience in New Zealand, in accord with New Zealand On Air's cultural brief to be "an independent leader in promoting local content and diversity in broadcasting". Over the period June 2006 to June 2007, New Zealand On Air granted $NZ14.68 million for locally-made Children and Young Persons programming.[16]

These special considerations bestow a distinctive status on the preschool audience, in that very young New Zealanders are excluded from deliberate targeting by television advertising. It is also acknowledgement of their membership – or more correctly, lack of membership – of instrumental constructions of the television audience through People Meter measurement and ratings. Children under the age of five years are not included in the 1,150 individuals who currently comprise the People Meter panel in New Zealand. The argument is that they are too immature to press the necessary buttons, to record viewing periods, nor cognizant of the purpose of such activities.

It could be argued that young children do not comprise a lucrative advertising market, with little recourse to direct purchasing. Nevertheless, many parents would argue that their children are increasingly influential in household decision-making. Arthur (2005) carried out parent interviews about their children's engagement with popular media culture. Parents concerns focused predominately on consumerism, stating they regularly felt under pressure to "purchase the latest toy, to take their child to fast food restaurants in order to get the latest promotional offer, and to buy their children clothing emblazoned with licensed characters and logos".[17] Other parents were concerned with popular media characters promoting special brands or food. As Arthur concludes, popular media culture situates young children as consumers.[18] Indeed, this had already been well established historically; Seiter[19] observed in the early 1990s how consumer culture was creating a separate peer culture and market, resulting in children being 'sold separately'. Buckingham[20] notes that there has been a continued blurring of the boundaries between entertainment, information and advertising, resulting in a 'consumer-media-culture',[21] which is especially widespread in television aimed at children. Arthur argues that the products linked to popular media culture are "sold" not just to children but also to the parents, who want to provide the best for their children.[22]

The combination of special age status and absence from commercial calculation means that preschool television has attracted little research attention in New Zealand. One notable exception is Lealand (1995) *Television and New Zealand Preschoolers: A Longitudinal Study*, which investigated the relationship between pre-school television and young viewers through cycles of repeated observations.[23] However, this research is now a decade old. The demographic and social shifts described above, suggest that updated research is needed.

Structural and technological changes are presenting significant challenges to the mediascape. Pay channels such as Nickelodeon have introduced competition for the youngest audience, and producers are being expected to extend content across a variety of platforms. In late October 2008, for example, Disney announced plans to extend its presence on pay-TV in New Zealand.[24] In the face of such changes, television in New Zealand continues to endeavour to provide its youngest citizens with the best of imported preschool programming, together with a significant local contribution designed for the changing demographics of the population. This is especially in respect to bi-culturalism (the relationship between Maori and European New Zealanders) but also multi-culturalism, the rapidly expanding Asian and Pacific Island sectors of the population.

Notes

1. Lemish, D. (2007) *Children and Television: A Global Perspective*. Oxford: Blackwell Publishing, p. 1.
2. Cotterell, G., von Randow, M., & Wheldon, M. (2008) An Examination of the Links between Parental Educational Qualifications, Family Structure and Family Wellbeing, 1981-2006. http://www.educationcounts.govt.nz/publications/assessment/32057/32056 Accessed 20 October 2008.
3. Prasad, R. (2005) The Families Commission. What Is It and What Can It Achieve? Paper presented to the 9th Australian Institute of Family Studies Conference, Melbourne, 9-11 February.
4. Pool, I., Dharmalingam, A., & Sceals, J. (2007) *The New Zealand Family from 1840: A Demographic History*. Auckland University Press: Auckland, p. 386.
5. Buckingham, D. (2003) *Media Education. Literacy, Learning and Contemporary Culture*. Cambridge: Policy Press.
6. Broadcasting Standards Authority (2008) *Seen and Heard: Children's Media Use, Exposure, and Response* Wellington: Broadcasting Standards Authority, p. 3.
7. 19% of 4-5 year-olds in NZSEI 1 and 2 watch video tapes or DVDs, compared to 89% in NZSEI 3 and 4 and 64% in NZSEI 5 and 6, Broadcasting Standards Authority, 2008, p. 46.
8. http://www.educationcounts.govt.nz/statistics/ece/ece_staff_return/licensed_services_and_licence_excempt_gr
9. Of these, 5.5% (10,580) were under the age of one, 13.8% (26,401) were one year of age, 20.3% (38,829) were two years of age, three year olds made up 29.4% (56,171), four year olds made up 30% (57,180) and 0.9% (1,746) were five year olds. In New Zealand children start primary school when they turn 5, although legally they are not required to do so until age 6. http://www.educationcounts.govt.nz/statistics/ece/ece_staff_return/licensed_services_and_licence_exempt_gr
10. Prasad, R. (2005) The Families Commission. What Is It and What Can It Achieve? Paper presented to the 9th Australian Institute of Family Studies Conference, Melbourne, 9-11 February.
11. Ministry of Social Development (2004) *The Social Report 2004*. Wellington: Ministry of Social Development.
12. New Zealand Census 2006.
13. John Rogers (2008) 'Jane and the Dragon' Literate Kids TV, www.sfgate.com/cgi-bin/article.cgi?f=/n/a/2008/03/03/entert. Accessed 1 October 2008.
14. ibid
15. Advertising on Television – Getting it Right for Children. www.nztbc.co.nz/children_tv/index.html. Accessed 9 October 2008.
16. New Zealand on Air Annual Report 2006-2007. Wellington: NZOA, 2007.

17. Arthur, L. (2005) 'Popular Culture: Views of Parents and Educators', in J. Marsh (Ed.), *Popular Culture, New Media and Digital Literacy in Early Childhood*, pp. 165-182. Abingdon, Oxon: RoutledgeFalmer, p. 170.
18. As above.
19. Seiter, E. (1993) *Sold Separately: Children and Parents in Consumer Culture*. New Brunswick, NJ: Rutgers University Press.
20. Buckingham, D. (2000) *After the Death of Childhood*. Cambridge: Polity Press in association with Blackwell Publishers.
21. Kenway, J., & Bullen, E. (2001) *Consuming Children: Education, Entertainment, Advertising*. Buckingham: Open University Press.
22. Arthur, L. (2005) 'Popular Culture: Views of Parents and Educators', in J. Marsh (Ed.) *Popular Culture, New Media and Digital Literacy in Early Childhood*, pp. 165-182.
23. See 'Where do Snails Watch Television? Preschool Television and New Zealand Children', in S. Howard (Ed.) *Wire-Up: Young People and the Electronic Media*, London: UCL Press, 1998.
24. Drinnan, J. (2008) 'Disney Out to Bolster Local Kids' TV market', *New Zealand Herald*, Oct 28, B3.

Preschoolers and the Internet in Sweden

Olle Findahl

Today, families with children represent the best equipped group in Sweden when it comes to media technology. Almost everyone in Sweden, 94 percent, has Internet access, which means that children and young people are growing up in an environment where the Internet is an integral part of the everyday life of the family (Findahl, 2008). They have good opportunities to learn to use new media technology nearly as soon as they start to walk.

In 2008 every fifth (21%) three-year-old has used the Internet, and among five-year-olds the proportion has grown to half (51%). Among nine-year-olds the proportion of Internet users is over 90 percent and from eleven years of age it is difficult to find someone who does not use the Internet (Findahl & Shemic, 2008).

Use of the Internet among preschoolers is limited, however, and it is only from ten years on that the majority have become daily users. The highest proportions of daily users are found among teenagers, with a peak at 16 years. This frequent usage continues up to the age of 30.

Method

In the annual study "The Swedes and the Internet", a representative sample of 2,264 individuals over the age of 12 years were interviewed by telephone in 2008. Those who were parents (471) of children between three and 12 years (779) were also asked questions about their children's use of the Internet.

Results

Almost all children in Sweden today have access to the Internet at home, and they start getting acquainted with the computer as a means to reach new worlds earlier and earlier. This trend toward an earlier beginning of Internet use has

Diagram 1. Frequency of Internet use in different age groups in Sweden 2008 (%)

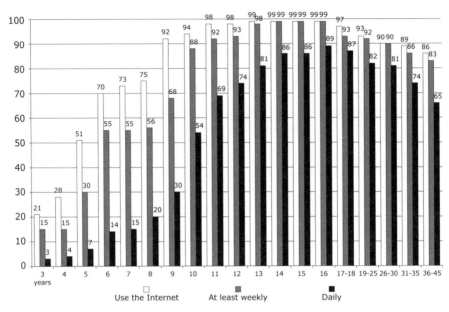

Source: The Adult survey, Parents survey and Youth survey. World Internet Institute 2008.

accelerated in recent years. If we look at age and use the measure of when 50 percent of an age group has started to use the Internet in some way, that age was ten years in 2002. Three years later, in 2005, the critical age had decreased to eight years. After another three years, in 2008, this age is now five years.

First phase (3-6 years): Games and Video

Many children have their first contact with the Internet when their parents connect to *Bolibompa*, the website for children by the Swedish public service television company, SVT. For them, even three-year-olds, *Bolibompa* is already familiar. They recognize the program and recurring characters from children's programs on television. On the *Bolibompa* site, the children are offered videos and various games that they can control by clicking. Some games are interactive educational. Popular videos can be replayed and watched many times. However, the time spent on the Internet among preschoolers is still limited.

Help from parents or older siblings is initially necessary to get things to work, but the most basic games and the selection of films can be controlled with clicks. The next step is for the child to enter his or her name, or to get help doing it. Names and symbols are often combined.

All these opportunities are being used more and more as online use becomes a habit, from more occasional use to regular use of the Internet at least a few times a week. Gaming has now become the dominant activity.

Diagram 2. The content of children's Internet use as their parents see it

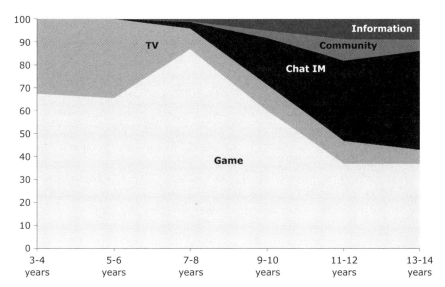

Source: Parents Survey, World Internet Institute 2008.

Second phase (7-10 years): More and more communication

When the children reach school age and have learned to read, a whole new world opens up for them – not only books and newspapers but also the Internet. They can search for information and find ads, but above all, they can write. They can keep in touch with their friends via instant messaging; communicating via the Internet is an increasingly frequent activity, while children still continue playing games as well. The nature of the games changes, and some are aware of more complicated games such as *World of Warcraft*, an online role-playing game for multiple players. Video viewing has declined. At the same time the world of communities is opening up, with social communities but also more special interest communities like *Star Doll* for fashion enthusiasts and *The Stable* for those interested in horses. Some are also using the Internet for help with their homework, even if school plays only a minor role for most children in elementary school among their Internet activities. There are no differences in access and use between boys and girls, even if there are differences in what boys and girls do online. These differences become more evident when the children grow older.

Third phase (11-14 years): Communication and communities

Among eleven-year-olds, three of four have become daily users of the Internet and their use is becoming more diverse. Many continue with gaming, but chatting with friends is of at least the same volume, and interest in online communities is increasing, although it will still be some years until the extensive interest in communities has spread to everyone. Some align themselves with Facebook while others upload pictures to Bilddagboken (The Picture Diary). Some have an interest in buying and selling things, and many start using the Internet in school.

Summary

The diffusion of the Internet among children does not follow the ordinary diffusion models. They themselves cannot decide to start using the Internet, but they can indirectly persuade their parents to invest money in a computer and an Internet connection. Most families with children belong to the early majority who are already online, but there are still parents with no interest in the Internet and low-income families who have problems affording an Internet connection. What seems now to be happening in many families with children is an increasing interest, and sometimes pressure, to get an online connection for younger and younger children.

However, the most fundamental changes during the past seven years have happened to children aged around seven, when they start school. Very few in this age group were using the Internet in 2002, whereas today 80-90 percent are online. These changes have happened not at school but at home.

If we use as a measure the age at which 50 percent of an age group has started to use the Internet in some way, this age was ten years in 2002. Three years later, in 2005, it had decreased to eight years. After another three years, in 2008, the critical age is now five years. And among three-year-old children, one in five has been online.

Literature
Findahl, O. (2008) *Internet and the Swedes 2008*. Gävle: World Internet Institute.
Findahl, O., & Shemic, S. (2008) *Young Swedes and the Internet 2008*. Gävle: World Internet Institute.

Additional Interviews

Interview with Daniel Anderson

According to your experience conducting research with young children, is television in some aspects good or bad for preschoolers?

It depends on the age of the child, but in this country (USA) from about age two and a half years on, there is good evidence that educational television programs are quiet effective at increasing children's knowledge and even some cognitive skills. This is for shows that are designed to do so, because in purely entertainment shows there is little obvious value other than to keep children occupied and entertained. On the other hand, we certainly know that children are in some way damaged by shows that incorporate a lot of violence.

And what about programs aimed at infants, like Baby Mozart?

We are talking here about children under two years of age: I think that the evidence is so far mostly negative, in the sense that the programming has no positive effect or that it may even have a negative effect on these children. The main reason for that is that at this point there is very little evidence that children under two years of age understand what they see. It is very hard to make these programs educational for babies.

Maybe following the music…

It can be useful for a parent to show babies such a thing because parents need to keep a baby occupied – perhaps while taking a bath or making supper or something of the sort. In the US many of these programs are marketed as educational or expecting that they will improve the baby's intellectual development and there is simply no evidence of that yet.

The CSA,[1] the French regulator, banned TV programs aimed at children under three…

Yes, I think that's a decision that resembles what we actually do. We use age two as a cutoff, because we do have evidence that children are beginning to understand and follow television after they are two years old. This makes it possible for programs to be educational for children between two and three years of age.

Your research on background television focuses on quizzes, but what would happen for instance if background TV is about violent news? We have seen in Chile, that 6 year olds, even when they are talking and playing with siblings and not paying any attention to the screen while their parents watch the news, they afterwards draw mostly violent scenes...

Yes, and that is particularly for older children. Older children will readily imitate violent behaviors, and incorporate those ideas to their thinking – about society and social relationships. That ends being bad to children in many ways. But because infants often don't really understand what they are seeing, those programs probably will not have that same kind of influence. Disturbing images may be understood by an older child and they might upset them. But the general idea of our research is that background television is quite disruptive to the child's playing behavior and certainly more research is needed in this field.

So we don't know if infants could get upset about the news...

The evidence we have on that is that the news show images that are frightening by themselves, then children can get very upset if they show for example a violent fight or a car accident or a bloody body or something of the like. We know that certainly three years old for example can recognize what he sees and can be very disturbed by that. Older children are more likely to be disturbed by stories of, for example, kidnapping or things that they think may happen to them or to their parents. But the very young children would be disturbed by things they can actually see.

Let's go to a completely different topic: do you think that background TV could be a preparation for 'multitasking' that is, doing several things at the same time?

We just don't know, I think it is a possibility but it is going to take more research where we actually follow children as they develop, to find out.

Do you think that media education is relevant for preschool kids?

Yes, I think so, particularly for young children: by the time children are about four years old, they start to ask questions about television, about what they are seeing, and so sometimes they ask questions such as "do you know this?", "why did that happen?", or "why did that person do that thing on television?". Or they might ask questions about: "can I have that?" or asking an older person what's going to happen next... And then when children are a little older – about five or six – they begin to ask a lot of questions about what's real on television and so there are really great opportunities for a parent or even an older sibling to teach children about what they are watching, so that children get a better understanding about media.

In our research we have met a three year old saying "this doll is not a real Barbie because it doesn't have 'Mattel' written on it"...

Yes, that's the beginning of a very important kind of learning...

Television is very powerful with children, it can be powerful in a good way and in a bad way, and parents should not just think of it as purely entertainment, because TV is a "teacher" and can teach children good things and also bad things. In my own opinion television probably has more impact on preschool children than on any other age.

Why is that?

The main reason is that – at least in USA – television is really the medium that preschoolers use the most. At about two and a half or three years of age, they start to spend a lot of time watching television, and as they begin to understand it, they really absorb a great deal of information; but they don't have the criteria yet to really question what they are watching, so they accept what they see on television as simply a part of the world. Older children are being influenced by other media, they begin to be able to read and start to become influenced by, for example, comic books, *anime*, but also computer games and the Internet. Preschool children don't use those media as much as they watch television. Television loses its power of being very important when children start going to school, but it still can be very influential to an older child.

Our findings show that around half of the mothers of babies are watching TV while breast feeding...

This is very common; I think it's very similar in the US. There is very little research with children less than twelve months of age, in relation to TV and video. We do know that, beginning at about six months of age, children can recognize some images on video screens, and we know that between six and twelve months old some of them, not all of them, like to watch baby videos. But we still have almost no evidence that they are learning anything from these videos, as I said earlier. And in several studies, of children under two years of age including infants less than one year of age, the more they are exposed to videos the worse they do in terms of cognitive development and attention development. Part of the reason comes from the sort of thing that we found in our research, and that is that television could be very distracting and disrupt to the child. We also found that when the TV set is on, parents are distracted and the interaction with their child turns to be of a much lower quality.

Note
1. Conseil Supérieur de l'Audiovisuel. www.csa.fr

Interview with Víctor Fuenmayor

What role does media literacy play in society?

You could say that the media, with all the variety of content they transmit – for example, information, reality shows, cartoons, etc. – are of truly enormous importance in terms of the amount of time they invade the imagination of viewers. Not only educational content, such as news or issues addressed in television programs; we also have to consider that television and the media educate as a global force that leads individuals to think, think about themselves, and develop as human beings in a more general sense. In that regard, I believe the media's reach is even broader than formal or institutional education, and in light of this we should change education so as to be able to understand the media, while looking at what the media have to offer for education.

What is the value of teaching media literacy to preschoolers, from the time they begin watching television or talking?

It is a fact that children are in contact with the media at a very early age, from day care on, but what needs to be done is to create a relationship with the media in which the child can have contact with all types of media. There would have to be a classification of all the stages of child development, since in their pre-verbal stage they already understand media communication. Parents and specialized institutions should establish a set of programs to be used in schools. There are a number of television programs that employ almost pre-verbal language through sounds, and children respond to them very well. Children get used to a schedule in which they may watch a TV program, and that could be a sort of initiation. However, we must take into account that children need movement, and programs – particularly in maternal schooling – should consider the influence of images, movement and sounds that, to me, could be a means of creating artistic awareness.

This is something you spoke about in New York, about the importance of having children learn from early on all types of expressions: artistic, dance, media, speech…

Exactly. It's like preparing them at a very early age, because almost all contemporary arts, as well as messages transmitted through television, movies and the Internet are messages we could call synthetic techniques; that is, there is not one sole expression. This is different than what some schools do, which is to teach children only through art, basically painting, for example. All expressions should be included, and then, in the case of the media, they can approach photography and the interpretation of photography, and early on introduce children to the interpretation of images in relation to other expressions, such as music, dance, etc.

What do you suggest regarding programs that are adequate for preschoolers? Obviously they are what helps children relate to their bodies, to sing, dance or express themselves...

Exactly, because early child education also has to do with learning through movement, exploring space, body, movement. They are like very vague codes, superior to synthetic techniques... For example, the child who almost falls asleep while watching television is symptomatic, because he or she has little interest in the image. If we consider this from an educational perspective, certainly there are activities that may be broadcast on television that the child can carry out at the same time. These are very important stages. Children are going from the domain of their imagination to mastering what is symbolic, the domain of what is real, "the construction of reality". In Barcelona, there have been experiences in media production with children in which they are provided cameras, and with the help of the cameras create television images. These children are amazed at the change between what they have seen first-hand and what is projected in images. I believe this is very important at an early age. I belong to UNISCOLA, the Catalan Municipal School of Expression and Psychomobility. It is not a very global experience in terms of education, but there are people in charge of child creativity, involving children under six years of age. It is a school for teachers, educators, psychologists and parents, and offers courses and workshops.

Would media literacy among children mean they would have greater independence, social inclusion and participation, even among minority children, such as indigenous cultures or other minorities in our countries?

First, we have to think about integration. Through their contact with their own culture they may relate to other cultures, with all their surrounding context. For example, I live in Maracaibo (in Venezuela) and have contact with the Wuayuu children in north Maracaibo, or I may have contact with Bari children. For them, the media are another world – some of them live in almost desert areas and others live in the jungle. They should be taught, but not under so much pressure that it becomes a menace to their indigenous traditions. A Mexican anthropologist explained to me that the same thing happens in Mexico. When Commander Marcos went from Chiapas to Congress, he wanted to speak at the Congress building itself, personally. In other words, he did not accept a spokesperson or another language that wasn't his own indigenous language. We have to speak about the media within the context of their cultural and world views. Television and media literacy could be introduced among the Wuayuu in Venezuela from the perspective of what could be called an oneiric education, because they believe strongly in symbols and dreams. This would be an educational strategy that wouldn't work among the Bari people who live in jungle areas, for example, because their world view is much more concrete. For them, movies and television are white people's dreams. In some Amazon regions, certain indigenous communities have difficulty understanding Spanish. Therefore, presence is important and language is presential. They don't consider audiovisual images, or anything transmitted through non-presential means, to be real. So you can see how there can be a positive relationship with the media, in terms of teaching, with the Wuayuus for example, but also a negative one, because it is not a relationship with something real, as is the case with the Baris.

You've already mentioned the role of the family in promoting media literacy. Do you believe that it is the context, or that all contexts, including the mother and the family, should contribute to media education in this technological era?

Currently, all contexts, and they are even being used in psychological therapy. When a child undergoes therapy, even individual therapy, there is a triangulation. You can't have a child in therapy without involving the parents or the child's formal education context. Using the media in an educational way is essential, as it also is to create this triangulation between the child-parents-school, tutor, teacher or whatever you want to call it. Media literacy education at school without the family, where children can watch all sorts of programs without precaution, is counterproductive. When children socialize they always have a counterpart, and there is a stage at which children are limited to their families. But there is also a stage at which the child may feel lonely and believe that media is the solution. However, this television distraction, in this case, may "uneducate". No institution can do anything by itself, because family ties must be strengthened, and the school and others as well as the children themselves must contribute to this. If not, it would not be effective.

Does a child's curiosity influence his or her exploration of mass media?

I believe so, because by reproducing the same media behavior of their family, such as zapping, they can find programs you would think children wouldn't be interested in. This happened to me with a documentary on whales, for example. I thought the boy wasn't interested, but he actually was, and just needed to be guided on the topic. Children have an enormous curiosity. Before they are seven, they go through a period of great creativity, and curiosity is what opens the door for them to what we could call imaginary or artistic creation – with images and with everything, because in the end, creativity is part of curiosity.

47

Interview with Angharad Valdivia

From your perspective, what is the relevance of television in the socialization of preschoolers?

Research in this area must be very careful because there is a lot of exposure to television among preschoolers, although it is not the same across all classes and ethnicities. Research in the United States shows that the upper middle class is very interested in retaining upward social mobility and children do not watch as much television as other groups of children, and parents and guardians are very much involved in what it is they watch. So, for example, broadcast television is not something these children would be exposed to much because their parents are more involved in engaging in more sophisticated types of programming. However, this is a small segment of the audience, and I would argue that they are the most powerful segment; they are the people who are running the country.

Most children are exposed to quite a lot of television and there are therefore implications in terms of their being socialized into cultural norms, and also in terms of their relating to other children in their social groups. So, for example, some of the research suggests that there are parents who do not allow their children to watch television; these children are not able to engage socially with other children. The non-TV-watching children miss out on a kind of common sense of the world in that children are making sense of each other and relating to each other in relation to this. In terms of preschoolers, then, I would argue that the research is still not conclusive because, depending on the situation and all sorts of other variables, some children rely much more on television than others do. So we're still going back to George Gerbner's kinds of findings about a heavy television diet. But this also applies to children, I would say, because children with heavier television diets experience different effects than do children with light television diets. I don't think it is irrelevant; television is quite relevant for children, and it's more so in certain situations, especially those in which television is being used almost as a babysitter, almost as a prevalent pastime rather than as a component of a much more diverse diet of activities and cultural input for children.

In Chile the situation is such that people belonging to the lower classes say that television is very good because it prevents children from going outside to play where there is sometimes violence or other social problems, and it's a way to keep them inside the home where they are safe. Is this the case in the US?

I think this is very interesting because basically it is about the concept of keeping them off the streets, and actually, that's what people say for upper middle-class kids, too – it keeps them off the streets. Especially in urban areas, you don't want your kids to be polluted by whatever urban perils there are out and about. Of course in an upper middle-class city you would keep them off the streets by having them take piano lessons, tennis lessons or whatever, but you would certainly keep them inside the home in a safe space. This would apply to any class, but some scholars would argue that in some situations the home itself is a very problematic and unsafe space. We cannot assume that the home is the ultimate safe space for most children, because what we find in media studies is that in terms of situations of duress, whether it be an economic downturn or a situation of war, or situations like that, all those external issues are deployed inside the home. So, for example, in situations of economic duress for the working class, or even the class that's not working – the fourth class – there is a lot more violence in the home as a result of this. So you're keeping kids at home but they are likely to be exposed to violence in as well as outside the home. I'm ambivalent about this, because how do you protect children when television is not strong enough to protect them from cultural violence in the inner city?

And maybe that does not apply to preschool children...?

You're talking about infants, right? Two or three years old. In terms of developmental research on children they are learning so much at this time, and one of the reasons I wanted to make a caveat or cautionary statement is that for all children, even those at this early age, for great amounts of time television will be influential. So if they're watching a lot of television it will be highly influential. Children process knowledge in a different way at this age, and if they're going out and about and witnessing whatever, that will also be highly influential. I am thinking of children who may be in violent households, watching TV content with a great deal of violence and then going out in the streets and witnessing violence.

Do you think programs aimed at preschoolers have social importance or are socially relevant?

It is an incredibly high-learning age. Media studies of children in the media show that children will be influenced by any input of knowledge at this time; the reason they are influenced more by more violent media is because there is more violent media; it's not necessarily because they are more influenced by violence than by other kinds of messages. So the challenge has been and continues to be to make non-violent media as visual, as oral, as seductive as violent media. The production of non-violent messages should be as visually alluring to them as the prod of violent messages. So there is social importance because at this age children are learning social cultural ethical parameters that will be influential to them for the rest of their lives. The importance for adults is that if children are going to be consuming a lot of media, if they are going to be consuming a lot of television, then we need to produce material that is as seductive and alluring to them as the stuff already being produced that's violent or antisocial, if you go by the parameters of television production.

And children under six or seven years of age are watching this type of program with violent content?

Yes, I think preschoolers are watching whatever is on and especially anything that is visually alluring – they'll watch that. In a sense, their brains are working at a much higher level than ours are; they have more brain cells and they are actually making growing connections, while our brains are actually decreasing. In a sense they're much more able to take in information. The research suggests that if the TV is on and the kid is there, they're going to pay attention to it. Especially once they are over 18 months or so, they will pay attention. Now, how they make sense of that? Well, that is a challenge. Scholars have decided that it has an accumulative long-term effect. We will never develop unless we pay attention, so if there is something that is a bit different they will pay attention to that. So if there's an over-abundance of a certain type of programming, then this is what has the greater effect; but it's not necessarily because it is special – rather just because it is more available and that's what you have more exposure to.

Do you think the programs aimed at these age groups have gender content and diversity aimed at integrating them?

The commercial TV wisdom has been that little girls are going to watch whatever the boys watch, whereas little boys will not watch anything that has anything to do with little girls, and that's where the big tie-ins [product placements] are. I'm talking about commercial television, because commercial television does not care about children; it doesn't really care about human beings in a sense. Commercial television is about the circulation of products, so it just cares about exposing audiences to products that will then continue to be sold to finance the production of television. I do think one of the things that can be done, and is being done, in terms of some of the marketing of commercial television in the United States and in other places, is that marketers are beginning to figure out that, for example, little girls are part of the audience and can actually generate product consumption perhaps at a greater level than little boys can. Because little girls are theorized by market culture to be the consumers of society because women are, and some consumption practices begin as early as preschool age, the market wants to begin it at an earlier and earlier age.

I think commercial television is also beginning to acknowledge that we live in a multicultural and very heterogeneous world, and that is another way to maximize profit and attract previously ignored audiences as well as hopefully

51

previously ignored disposable incomes. And they are programming in the hopes of capturing this audience. And again, in the realm of commercial television, none of this really is done because they care about children, because they care about minorities, or because they care about the disabled. It's done to find new markets to generate new avenues of profit. This opens up a whole age for non-commercial television. For example, in the US *Sesame Street* has been around since the early days and has been heavily criticized for some of the strategies they have undertaken, but they've included women, they've included people of color and issues of age, and despite heavy criticism, although I support them, they included the theme of death – because people die – earlier on. But again, this was not done on commercial television. However, *Sesame Street* cannot be regarded as the ultimate output of non-commercial television, as it has an incredible branding and commercialization of its characters.

Do you think it is important for very young children to receive media education or media literacy, or something of the sort?

Yes, I think media literacy can start as early as you start watching television with your kids. Again, kids are incredibly smart. They're learning so they will learn from watching massive hours of *The Powerpuff Girls*, for example, and you know it's incredibly violent, and people say "Hey, it's girl power, it's great!". But where do you go to find more violence per minute in any show? So people think it's gender equity, and yes it is. You do have little girls going out there and kicking butt. Yet it's incredibly violent. As much as any show.

Going back to media literacy, kids are watching television from the moment they can communicate with you, and one of the most useful things coming out of media studies is that kids are going to watch television, and you can ostracize them by not letting them watch it; they will not be in the same universe as the rest of their friends. Actually, Andrea Press' book *Women Watching Television* introduces a number of women whose parents didn't let them watch television when they were young and they all became high achieving professionals, but all of them said they wished they had been allowed to watch TV. They really felt like outcasts while they were growing up; they were real outsiders. They did not fit in, and it was harsh to grow up that way, to be the only little girl who couldn't talk about what the other little girls were talking about.

But to return to media literacy; when you watch television with your little children, think about what to ask. You can ask them little questions like where are all the mommies, or whatever. You can start at a very basic level and build on that, and by the time your child gets to kindergarten you can have a media critic. In some places like England, media literacy is introduced very early on, and I mean not at college but in elementary school. I have a friend who is also a scholar who has three boys of the same age, and she has been going to their classroom once a week to read them classic fairy tales and then give them a transnational, feminist, multiethnic reading of these fairy tales. Teachers don't have the time to do this.

So media literacy is just like teaching literacy; we need to include it personally as parents and we also need to engage in activism to include it in the curriculum.

Do you think media literacy is just a tool for preventing negative effects on children, or could it integrate children in society? Not just to protect, but a tool for more participation?

Definitely, using it just as a means to protect them from negative effects takes us back to a media paradigm that has been largely discounted within media studies. It's almost a transmission model. But, certainly, it can really empower everybody. I would also encourage people to engage more in production, as we move into the era of convergence. Even 20 years ago, to say we were engaging in more production was really a lie because to engage in production you needed professional training; you had to go into the huge media industries. But now with the convergence of technology, digital technology, access to e-mail, and fairly inexpensive production facilities, you already see people being very creative and building on critical media literacy to do this. Because media is intertextual and media literacy allows you to take what's there and turn it into something else. It then… I think it provides a participatory vision of the subject in relation to media.

Relating media literacy to gender issues…

There's a book that's just come out called *The Lolita Effect*. There's a whole new world of Girl Studies. It's a new area of studies. I am a reviewer of *Choice Magazine* and in charge of reviewing books in this area of study.

There are many books that have come out that say we have to protect little girls from television, and that little girls are overexposed to sexuality. They listen to music with hypersexualized lyrics, and probably don't even understand them. We have to engage in media literacy in relation to them and their sexuality, and a lot of people say we can't expose children to sexuality. It's too early in their childhood, or it's too late in their teens. We have to engage in some kind of age-appropriate media literacy that includes tools for helping children deal with hypersexualized messages. Media literacy that includes these types of tools is controversial because people say it's too early – that it's the hypersexualization of little girls. But Gigi Durham [author of *The Lolita Effect*] says it's never too early. You really have to provide little girls with the tools so that they have a healthy sexuality and not a shameful effect.

Authors and Interviewees

Daniel Anderson
Ph.D., Professor
Department of Psychology
University of Massachusetts Amherst
Amherst
USA

Patricio Cabello
M.A., Former Researcher at Chilean
National Television Council (CNTV)
Ph.D. Candidate
Universidad Complutense de Madrid
Madrid
Spain

Olle Findahl
Ph.D., Professor
World Internet Institute
Gävle
Sweden

Víctor Fuenmayor
Ph.D., Honoris Causa Doctor
University of Zulia
Maracaibo
Venezuela

Juan Enrique Huerta
Ph.D., Research Chair on Media
Communications
Universidad de Monterrey
Monterrey
México

Geoff Lealand
Associate Professor
Screen & Media Studies
Waikato University
Hamilton
New Zealand

Mary Jane Shuker
Senior Lecturer
School of Education Policy and Im-
plementation
Victoria University of
Wellington College of Education
Wellington
New Zealand

María Dolores Souza
Head of the Research Department
National Television Council (CNTV)
Santiago
Chile

Angharad Valdivia
Ph.D., Professor in Communications
University of Illinois at Urbana-
Champaign
Urbana-Champaign
USA